conte

GW00992770

guidelines & equipment

age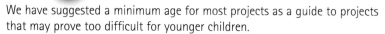

We have suggested a minimum age for most projects as a guide to projects that may prove too difficult for younger children.

ALL AGES means from two years upwards but these projects still require supervision. The ages given are a guide only, as children differ in their ability to master certain steps. With close supervision, younger children may be able to manage more difficult projects, although their attention span may not last until the project is finished. We have used the word **'Adult'** to show where help will be needed for very young children, or where toxic products or sharp instruments are to be used, or where cooking or heating is required.

safety first

Activities that involve small objects, such as polystyrene, beads and buttons should be kept for older children, over five years. There is a high risk that younger children will put these objects into their mouths, ears or noses.

Before buying or using craft materials check labels to ensure that all felt-tipped pens, crayons, play dough, paints and glues are non-toxic. Play dough can be made at home with edible dye (see play dough recipes on page 4).

Supervise children using scissors to avoid cuts and wounds. Make sure all scissors are put away after use. Choose scissors with a blunt end or children's safety scissors or training scissors.

Supervise all use of string and cord so that children do not use it to cut off circulation or breathing.

Older children only should use needles and these should be blunt-ended. Keep pins and needles in a secure container away from children. Make sure all pins and needles are put away after use to avoid nasty accidents.

Supervise all washing up of tools after use. Water is dangerous and children can drown in a small amount of water.

collecting & storing materials

These materials will be handy for collage, construction, painting, printing and many other children's crafts.

bark
beads & buttons
bottle tops
boxes & containers
bulldog clips
candles
cardboard sheets
cellophane
chenille sticks
clock parts
clothespegs
confetti
corks
corrugated cardboard
cotton reels
cotton wool
cylinders
egg cartons

fabric scraps
foam pieces
fur
greeting cards
postcards
hair curlers/hair pins
magazines
matchsticks
matchboxes
mesh
newspapers
old clean socks
old telephone books
orange & onion bags
paper & cardboard
paper clips
paper patty pans
pasta (dry)

plastic containers
polystyrene pieces
rubber bands
sandpaper
seeds
shaving brushes
shells
springs
squirt & spray bottles
sticks
straws
string
thread
toothpicks
wire
wire coat-hangers
wood off-cuts
wool

Store collage and craft materials in separate containers to avoid mixing them up. It can be a nightmare trying to separate hundreds of small items! Make collecting items fun and encourage children to think creatively about how they can expand their collections of collage and craft materials.

play dough recipes

play dough

you will need

1 cup salt

2 cups flour

4 teaspoons cream of tartar

2 tablespoons cooking oil

2 cups water

powder paint or vegetable dye
   or food colouring

saucepan

1 Mix all ingredients in saucepan.
2 **Adult:** cook on medium heat
   for three to five minutes,
   stirring constantly until mixture
   becomes stiff. Store in airtight
   container in refrigerator. It will
   last for quite a while and has
   the consistency of commercially
   prepared play dough. Additional
   colour may be worked
   into dough.

uncooked salt dough

This is the easiest recipe; it can be
made in less than three minutes. Let
children make the dough themselves
whenever possible. This recipe makes
enough for six children.

you will need

powder paint or vegetable dye or
   food colouring

2 cups flour

1 cup salt

1 tablespoon cooking oil

1 cup water

bowl

spoons

1 Mix powder paint or vegetable dye or
   food colouring with the flour and salt.
   Add oil and water.
2 Knead dough. Children will like to use
   rollers, biscuit cutters and toothpicks
   with dough. If it becomes sticky, add
   more flour. Dough will keep for more
   than a week, even longer if it is kept in
   the refrigerator but it has a tendency
   to crumble.

Small shapes of this mixture can be
baked in a 180°C (350°F) oven for
45 minutes to make them hard.

print pad

you will need

thin sponge
shallow tray

1 Place a sponge in the tray. Place several spoonsful of paint onto the sponge.
2 To print, just press the printing object onto the sponge. The sponge loads a minimum amount of paint, evenly distributed across the printing object, which helps to avoid smearing and gives a clear print. Make a cushion by placing a newspaper under the paper on which the print impression is to be made.

tips for staying clean

An old shirt or a garbage bag with the head and arm holes cut out will make a good cover-up to keep children's clothing clean.

Sheets of newspaper or old plastic shopping bags will protect the work surface and make cleaning up much easier.

Keep old rags and sponges handy for cleaning up. Shallow containers, such as ice-cream containers, are useful to hold water for painting and are less likely to be tipped over than tumblers.

Plastic lids from ice-cream containers make great paint palettes.

Soda water helps to break up and remove dry paint stains from carpet.

fingerpaint & glue recipes

cornflour paste

Add to ordinary paint or add food colouring to use as fingerpaint; use as an economical extender for paint; use as a paper glue or use in papier-mâché.

you will need

3 parts water (3 cups)

1 part cornflour (1 cup)

food colouring

saucepan

1 **Adult:** bring the water to boil in a saucepan. Remove from heat.

2 **Adult:** dissolve cornflour in a little cold water and add to hot water, stirring constantly. Boil until clear and thick (about one minute).

To make fingerpaint, add desired food colouring. This mixture will be very smooth. Offer it to the children while it is still warm to touch. A tablespoon of glycerine may be added to make it glossy. A ½ cup of Lux soap flakes may be added to give fingerpaint a lumpy texture.

Store in refrigerator as it spoils in hot weather.

flour paste

Useful for gluing collage and papier-mâché paper.

you will need

1 part water

1 part flour

food colouring

oil of cloves, wintergreen
  or peppermint

bowl

spoon

1 Pour water into bowl. Add flour, stirring constantly. Add food colouring. Salt may be added for a different texture.

2 Add a few drops of oil of cloves, wintergreen or peppermint as preservatives. Thin with cold water.

Store in airtight container in refrigerator. Longlasting.

starch

Very useful for gluing paper. It dries clear and sticks to glass, metal, waxed paper, plastics. Occasionally commercial-strength liquid starch is not thick enough.

you will need
1 part starch granules (1 cup)
2 parts boiling water (2 cups)
food colouring
saucepan

1 **Adult:** add a small amount of cold water (about 6 tablespoons) to starch granules to make a paste.
2 **Adult:** add boiling water to starch, stirring constantly. The mixture should become thick and milky glossy. If it doesn't thicken it is because the water isn't hot enough. Simply put it on the stove and bring it to the boil. Remove from stove.
3 Add food colouring. Add some glycerine to make mixture glossy and/or ½ cup of Lux soap flakes for a different texture. Give starch mixture to children while still warm.

Store in refrigerator as it spoils in hot weather.

homemade commercial-strength liquid starch
Dissolve 1 teaspoon of granulated starch in a small amount of water. While stirring, add 1 cup of hot water. Bring to the boil for one minute, stirring constantly. Cool.

Store in airtight container in refrigerator. Longlasting.

extra strong homemade liquid starch
Follow instructions for Homemade commercial-strength liquid starch (above), using 1 tablespoon of granulated starch instead of a teaspoon.

drawing & painting

easel painting

you will need
clothes pegs, bull-dog clips
    or adhesive tape
large sheet of paper
easel
paint in small bowls
long-handled paintbrushes
apron

1 **Adult:** peg, clip or tape the
  paper onto the easel.
2 Put on apron. Using lots
  of different colours, paint pictures on the paper.
3 Remove paper from easel and allow it to
  dry thoroughly.

tip Long-handled paintbrushes allow more freedom of
    movement, although short-handled brushes are much
    easier for younger children to use. When buying or
    making an easel, make sure the paint tray has an
    opening which makes cleaning easier. Sometimes a
    paint stand is more suitable. Two easels placed next to
    each other encourages interaction between children.

fabric designs

you will need
fabric crayons
white drawing paper
fabric (synthetic or a
    blend of polyester/
    cotton)
sheet of paper,
    if needed
iron

1 **Adult:** carefully read directions accompanying fabric crayons.
2 Using fabric crayons, draw a design or picture on the drawing paper on one side of the paper only. (Please note that the design will be reversed when transferred to the fabric.) Cut out the design.
3 **Adult:** following directions included in fabric crayons packet, transfer the design from paper to fabric. (If you are using a T-shirt or pillowcase, place plain paper inside to stop dye going through to fabric underneath.) Place design, right-side down on top of fabric. Take care not to move the design or a double image will result. Move iron evenly across design to prevent steam marks appearing on fabric. If the iron is left in the same spot for too long, colour will not result where the iron's steam holes have been sitting above the fabric.

Fabric crayons are available from art and craft supplies stores. Designs must be heat-sealed according to the manufacturer's instructions.

crayon etchings

you will need
crayons (light colours)
small sheet of paper
newspaper
black crayon
hairpin or end of a paintbrush

1 Pressing firmly to produce a thick layer of crayon, cover
all the paper with different coloured crayons. Place a
thick pad of newspaper under the sheet of paper. Cover
crayon picture with black crayon. The newspaper pad
helps the black crayon to cover the paper more evenly
but remove the newspaper pad for the etching, which
requires a hard surface.

2 Place paper on one layer of newspaper (to make clean-
up easier). Make another picture by scraping off the
black layer of crayon with the end of a hairpin or end
of paintbrush to reveal colours underneath.
(Any blunt instrument can be used to scrape off the
black layer. Use different blunt instruments for
different effects.)

magic painting

you will need
sheet of absorbent paper
long thin candle
thin paint in small bowl
brushes (shaving brushes are easy for small
  children to hold)
apron

1 Put on apron.
2 Draw on absorbent paper using either end of the
  candle depending on the desired effect.
3 Paint over the wax design using a brush and one
  or more colours. The wax design resists the paint
  and shows through clearly.

Try using crayons instead of candles; black is
most effective.

straw painting

you will need
non-absorbent paper
newspaper
food colouring mixed with water, or thin paint
spoon or paintbrush
straws
apron

1 Put on apron.
2 Place paper on newspaper-covered table. Put a
    little paint or food colouring on paper with spoon
    or paintbrush.
3 Point straw in direction you want paint to go; put
    straw to lips and blow. The paint will fan out to make
    interesting patterns the more you blow on the straw.
    (Do not breathe the paint in through the straw.)

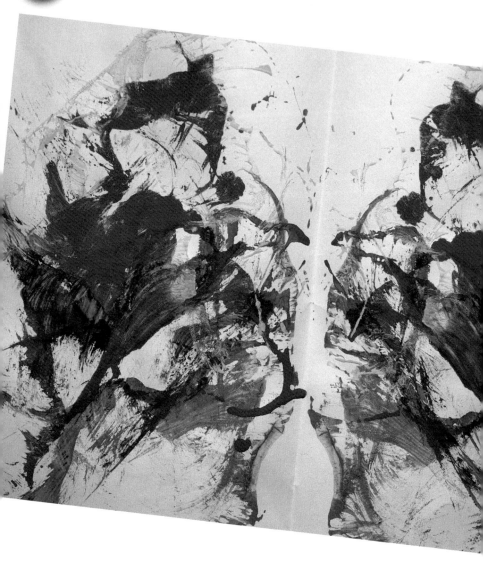

string painting

you will need
sheet of paper, folded in half
paint in shallow dishes
50cm (20in) lengths of string
apron

1 Put on apron.
2 Place pre-folded piece of paper beside paint tray.
  Open paper.
3 Drop one end of string into paint, keeping hold
  of dry end.
4 Pull string out of tray onto paper until paint-
  covered string is on paper and dry end of the
  string is at the edge of paper.
5 While still holding onto the string, carefully fold
  the paperon top of the string with your free hand.
6 Press down on paper and pull string out.
  Open paper.
7 Repeat with a new string dipped in a different
  colour. (Use separate strings for each colour.)
  For a different design, drag the string sideways
  around the paper while pulling it out.

After gaining a little experience with this
method, try using thick and thin paint and
mix it with some glue for a different effect.

bubble painting

you will need
dishwashing liquid
powder tempera paint or powder paint
straws
sheet of paper
empty cans or plastic containers
water
apron

1 Put on apron.
2 Pour ¼ cup of dishwashing liquid into container.
  In a separate container, mix small amount of water
  with paint.
3 Add paint mixture to dishwashing liquid until colour
  is intense.
4 Put straw into paint mixture and gently blow until the
  bubbles slightly flow over the top of the container.
  (Do not breathe the paint in through the straw).
5 Roll paper around gently on top of bubbles so as not to
  burst the bubbles. Try not to press the paper flat on top
  of the bubbles. Repeat the process with several colours
  for a pretty sheet of multi-coloured paper.
6 Allow paper to dry before using.

marble painting

you will need
marbles
paint in small bowls
sheet of paper
large cardboard box
straining spoon
bowls of water
apron

1 Put on apron.
2 Place marbles in paint bowls. Place paper in bottom of box.
3 Spoon a coloured marble into the box. Roll the marble around so that it leaves a coloured pattern on the paper. Take marble out with spoon and wash it in one of the bowls of water. Repeat with different coloured marbles.
4 Take the painting out of the box and hang to dry.

printing

leaf prints

you will need
leaves
cardboard
PVA glue
thin paint
shallow dish (about 1cm [3/8in] deep)
print roller
sheet of absorbent paper
spoon
apron

1 Put on apron.
2 Arrange leaves in desired design on the cardboard. Glue leaves onto cardboard and allow to dry.
3 Put a spoonful of paint into shallow dish. Move print roller through paint until roller is evenly coated. Roll paint onto leaves (a brush will not work).
4 Lay a piece of paper on top of the leaves. Rub the paper with a clean, dry hand. The raised veins and edges will make an impressive design. Take several prints from the same painting.

The same technique can be used with wire mesh, lace or netting instead of leaves.

OVER
2
YEARS

mesh dab-prints

you will need

plastic mesh bag (onion bags or pantihose)
foam, fibre filling or fabric scraps
print pads loaded with paint (see page 5)
paper
string
apron

1 **Adult:** make dabbers by filling plastic mesh squares or pantihose with foam, fibre or fabric scraps. Tie firmly with string.

2 Put on apron.

3 Press the dabber onto the foam print pad. Press dabber onto the paper. To avoid paint colours mixing, return dabbers to their original print pad.

play dough prints

you will need
play dough (see page 4)
tools (pencils, bottle caps, wire mesh, biscuit cutters,
    cooking utensils)
paint
print pad (see page 5)
paper

1 Roll play dough into a ball. Flatten it until it is about
  5cm (2in) thick.
2 On one side of the play dough, press any tools in to make a
  design. You can also draw on the play dough with a pencil
  or the end of a paintbrush.
3 Gently press play dough onto print pad, remove, press onto
  paper. Repeat with different colours and designs.

OVER 3 YEARS

29

OVER
3
YEARS

fruit & vegetable prints

you will need
oranges, lemons, potatoes, carrots, onions
paint
print pads (see page 5)
sheet of paper
knife
apron

1 **Adult:** cut fruit and vegetables in half to make a flat surface.
   Sometimes a fruit or vegetable must be allowed to drain
   upside down on a paper towel before it is able to absorb
   paint from the pad.
2 Put on apron.
3 Press printing object into print pad, remove, press onto
   paper. Repeat with different colours and different fruit
   and vegetables.

   Hand prints can also be made by pressing hand onto print
   pad and then onto paper. Children over five may be able
   to cut a pattern into a potato with a plastic knife, spoon or
   melon scoop to get an unusual print on paper.

spatter stencil

you will need
large cardboard box, if necessary
sheet of paper
adhesive tape, if necessary
pressed leaves, flowers or stencils cut out of cardboard
comb or piece of wire screen taped to an old picture frame
   or a box screen
old toothbrush or nail brush
thin paint in bowl
apron

1 Put on apron.
2 If working in a restricted space, or in the house where furniture
   may get damaged, get a large grocery box and cut out one side.
   Place sheet of paper inside box and tape edges down so that it
   will not shift.
3 Lay leaves, flowers, grasses or stencils on paper.
4 Hold comb or place piece of wire screen about 10cm (4in) above level
   of paper. Our photograph is of a box screen made for preschool or
   kindergarten use. It is easy to improvise with an old picture frame.
5 Dip toothbrush or nail brush into paint.
6 Draw the paint-filled brush many times across the flat side of the
   comb or across the screen. If the brush is loaded with paint, spatter
   drops will be big and coarse. A small amount of paint will produce a
   spray effect.
7 Allow paint to dry, then remove leaves and other decorations.

For a different effect, try the spatter technique by scraping a piece of
chalk over a screen held above glue or starch-covered paper.

OVER
4
YEARS

Ben. H.

OVER 3 YEARS

sponge prints

you will need
small thick sponges
clothes pegs
paint-loaded print pads (see page 5)
sheet of paper
scissors
apron

1 **Adult:** cut sponges into various shapes. Cut two slots in top of sponge, about 1cm ($^3/_8$in) deep and 3cm (1¼in) apart, for peg to clip into. Clip peg into slots in top of sponge to act as a handle. Two thin sponges can be glued together with PVA glue and used in the same way.
2 Put on apron.
3 Press sponge onto printing pad, then press sponge onto paper. Repeat process with different shapes and colours. This creates a very interesting textual effect.

collage & construction

skittles

newspaper
funnel
several empty
   plastic bottles
clean sand
paper paste or cornflour
   paste (see page 6)
paint in small bowls
paintbrushes
PVA glue
wool and other
   collage materials
clear gloss enamel

tip A fast and easy
   alternative is to papier-
   mâché the heads and
   necks only, then attach
   to bottles using strong
   tape. Apply paint and
   other decorations
   directly to the plastic
   bottles and the papier-
   mâché heads.

1 Crumple double sheets of newspaper into roughly
   round shapes for the heads, pulling out longish
   pieces for the necks.

2 Using a funnel, fill each plastic bottle about one-
   third full of sand. The sand helps prevent bottles
   from falling over too easily.

3 Push the newspaper necks and heads into the
   mouths of the bottles, ensuring there is a tight
   fit. Tear remaining newspaper into largish strips;
   dip strips into paper paste or cornflour paste so
   that they are covered all over with paste. Stick
   newspaper strips all over the heads and down onto
   the necks, to secure newspaper heads to bottles.
   Continue sticking newspaper strips to bottles until
   they are completely covered with two or three
   layers of newspaper. Allow bottles to dry for a
   few days.

4 Paint the heads of the bottles and allow to dry.
   Paint the bodies of the bottles in colourful designs;
   allow to dry.

5 Paint eyes, noses and mouths on heads; allow to
   dry. Glue wool on for hair and decorate bodies
   with collage materials; allow to set.

6 **Adult:** paint the bottles with clear gloss enamel;
   allow to dry.

Stand skittles up and try to knock them all over
with a ball.

OVER
4
YEARS

pea mobile

you will need
fresh pea pods
coloured toothpicks, preferably pointed at both ends
string

1 Shell peas.
2 Stick toothpick into pea. Place pea on the other end of toothpick and stick another toothpick into same pea. Continue this process to create a geometric structure. Take care that no more than four toothpicks are stuck into each pea because the pea will fall apart.
3 When finished, allow peas to dry out for several days. Do not touch them while they're drying.
4 Tie string to structure and hang mobile from ceiling.

chenille stick creatures

you will need
variety of chenille sticks, various colours,
with short or shaggy fur

1 Twist chenille sticks into interesting
animals and people. Odds and ends can
be used for eyes and clothes. Let your
imagination loose!

ALL
AGES

plastic cup flowers

you will need
coloured plastic cups
tissue paper or paper serviettes
stickers for decoration
drinking straws with bendable joint
vase, pot or branch
glue
adhesive tape
scissors

1 Using scissors, cut the rim off a plastic cup. Fringe the cup
   from the rim almost to the base, without breaking off the
   pieces. One cup can be glued inside another to make extra
   petals, if desired.
2 Gently bend the petals back. Crumple a piece of tissue paper
   or paper serviette and glue it into the base of the cup.
   Crumple tiny balls of a contrasting colour paper and glue
   them around the edge of the first paper centre. Decorate the
   flower with stickers.
3 Trim a drinking straw to desired size, tape to back of flower
   for the stem.
4 Arrange flowers in a vase or pot, or tape to a branch
   for display.

For variation, cut individual petal shapes from plastic cup or
plate and glue together at the flower centre. Use the base of a
second cup for the centre and fill with coloured cotton wool,
or decorate with stickers.

vegetable sculpture

you will need
coloured toothpicks
apples, oranges and
    various fruits
carrots, potatoes and
    various vegetables
sultanas, marshmallows,
    soft sweets, chenille
    sticks,to decorate

1 Using the toothpicks, stick
   a selection of fruits and
   vegetables together to form
   a sculpture or a creature.
   Choose foods that will be easy
   to stick toothpicks into; avoid
   hard foods. Vegetables could
   be cooked slightly so they are
   more easily pierced by the
   toothpicks. Decorate as desired.

salad clown

you will need
dinner plate (with a slight bowl works best)
mashed potato
lettuce leaves
hard-boiled egg slices
olive slices
chives
alfalfa
tomato
capsicum skin strip
carrot pieces
cucumber slices
knife

1 With a knife, spread mashed potato inside bowl of plate until smooth and flat.
2 Decorate clown with lettuce for hair, egg and olive slices for eyes, chives for eyelashes, alfalfa for eyebrows, end pieces of tomato for cheeks and nose, capsicum for mouth, cucumber slices for ears and carrot slices for bow tie. Let your imagination run wild!

collage kite

you will need
favourite painting or print
light-weight collage materials
string decorated with collage materials (for tail)
string
PVA glue
scissors

1 Cut a kite shape from an old painting or print.
2 Glue on any light-weight collage materials.
3 Tie on a tail made from any stringing materials.
  Tie a string on other end of kite. Hold on to
  string and run.

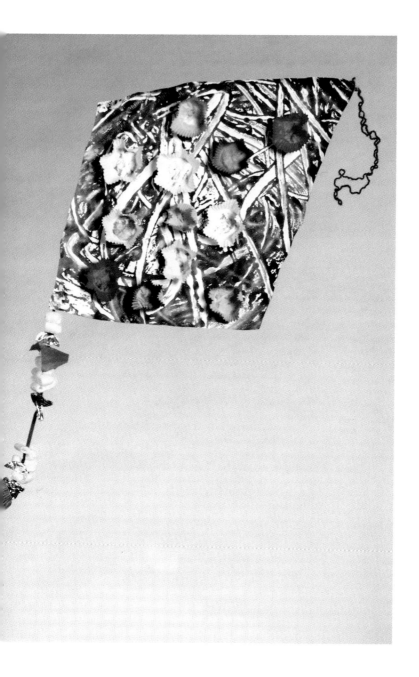

ALL
AGES

paper bag kite

you will need

large paper bag

paper ring reinforcements

string (2.4 metres or about 2½ yards)

paint in small bowls

paintbrushes

paper collage materials

tissue paper and crepe paper streamers

hole puncher

PVA glue

scissors

1 Punch hole on each of the four corners of the paper bag (at least 3cm [1¼in] from edge of bag). Put a paper ring reinforcement on each hole.

2 Cut two pieces of string to a length of about 80cm (about 2½ft). Tie each end of the string into an opposite hole to form two loops.

3 Cut a piece of string about 80cm (about 2½ft) long. Put it through the two loops and tie it. The string will act as a handle.

4 Paint paper bag kite as desired. Allow to dry.

5 Glue on paper collage materials and streamers. Allow to dry.

6 Open the paper bag kite. Hold onto the string and run so that the wind catches in the paper bag kite and makes it fly.

note Younger children will need help with steps 1, 2, 3.

pegs

you will need
wooden spring clothes pegs
paint in small bowl
paintbrush
felt-tipped pens
cotton wool, fabric scraps, crepe paper or wool
PVA glue

1 Paint peg any colour.
2 Draw on features with felt-tipped pens.
3 Glue pieces of cotton wool, fabric, crepe paper or
   wool to make a creature or person. There is no
   end of possibilities when making peg creatures:
   crocodiles, lions, Santa Claus, buildings, birds and
   clowns are just a few ideas.

ALL
AGES

53

play dough beads

you will need
¾ cup flour
½ cup cornflour
½ cup salt
vegetable dye or food colouring
bowl
90ml (3 fluid oz) warm water
toothpicks
clear gloss enamel

All play dough recipes may be used for jewellery, however those recipes made with salt tend to have a white residue which is particularly noticeable on dark-coloured play dough.

1 Mix first five ingredients in bowl. Add warm water gradually until mixture can be kneaded into a stiff dough. Dust with flour to reduce stickiness.
2 Mixture may be rolled into balls for beads. Pierce each bead with a toothpick then gently make circular movements to increase the size of the hole. Allow to dry for a few days. Large beads take longer to dry.
3 Holes should be checked after a day to see if they need punching. Paint if desired. This recipe makes a reasonably smooth dough that retains colour when dry. If desired, coat beads with clear gloss enamel to bring out colour.

box puzzle

you will need
child's drawing or painting
ruler
felt-tipped pen
empty matchboxes
PVA glue
scissors

1 Select a favourite drawing or painting, preferably one that is simple but solidly coloured.

2 **Adult:** using the ruler and the felt-tipped pen, mark off the matchboxes on the back of the drawing, making marks across the top and down the sides of the paper. Draw vertical and horizontal lines on the paper to join the marks and create matchbox shapes.

3 Using scissors, follow the lines and cut out the rectangles. Glue each piece of the drawing, right-side up, to the top of each matchbox. Arrange the boxes to match the original drawing.

ALL
AGES

plaster hands

you will need
casting plaster (available from hardware stores)
2 large ice-cream containers
powder paint
water
spoon
large paper clip
paper or plastic plate

1 Pour plaster powder into an ice-cream container (use about 500 grams (about 1lb) per hand). Make up two to three hands worth of plaster at a time.

2 Add paint powder. Add enough water to the plaster so the consistency seems rough and cracked but is smooth when a spoon is run over the top. Stir plaster thoroughly.

3 Bend open paper clip a little as illustrated and place near top of plate. Scoop plaster into plate, press down and smooth over.

4 Plaster is ready when it holds the shape of a finger when pressed into it. Plaster is usually ready as soon as it is put in the plate. Press hand into plaster and remove hand quickly.

5 Leave plaster overnight to harden. Remove from plate. Dig around paper clip a little and use it to hang on a nail in the wall.

papier-mâché bangles

you will need
cardboard
newspaper
paper paste
white powder tempera
    paint or sheet of
    white paper
powder paint in
    small bowls
felt-tipped pens
liquid starch
coloured tissue paper
clear gloss enamel,
    if desired
stapler
scissors

1 **Adult:** cut a cardboard strip about 28cm (11in) long and as wide as a bangle, about 2cm (¾in) to 4cm (1½in). Overlap the ends until the strip fits over the child's hand loosely, allow for thickness added by papier-mâché. Staple together the ends of the cardboard strip.

2 Tear newspaper into small strips about 2cm (¾in) x 6cm (2½ in). Dip a piece of newspaper into paper paste and wrap newspaper around the bangle. Repeat this process until the bangle has been covered all over with at least three layers of newspaper.

3 Cover the bangle with thin white paper; or if painting with white paint allow bangle to dry completely otherwise the newspaper will show through, especially if the bangle is glossed. It may take several days for the papier-mâché to dry. (Bangles may be placed in microwave on defrost cycle for 5-10 minutes to speed up drying).

4 Decorate bangles by painting or drawing on them or covering them with liquid starch and layers of coloured tissue paper.

5 **Adult:** when dry, paint with clear gloss enamel.

OVER
3
YEARS

stained glass window

you will need

black paper
same size sheets
  waxed paper,
  tracing paper or
  any transparent
  paper
cellophane or tissue
  paper torn into
  small pieces about
  3cm (1¼in) to
  8cm (3in)
liquid starch (if using
  tissue paper)
adhesive tape,
  if needed
PVA glue
scissors

1 **Adult:** fold the black paper into eighths. On a side that has only folds (no raw edges), cut out a square as illustrated. When unfolded this is the window frame.

 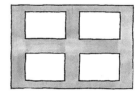

2 Place waxed paper or tracing paper onto table. If it curls, tape corners to table. If using tissue paper, apply a little liquid starch to waxed paper and place tissue paper on it. If using cellophane, put glue around edges and place it on waxed paper. Liquid starch will make cellophane buckle.

3 Glue frame onto the waxed paper or tracing paper. Hang on the window for the sun to shine through. Heavy white paper should replace the transparent paper if the picture is not to hang on a window.

index

Editorial director Susan Tomnay
Creative director Hieu Chi Nguyen
Designer Mary Keep
Director of sales Brian Cearnes
Marketing manager Bridget Cody
Production manager Cedric Taylor

Chief executive officer Ian Law
Group publisher Pat Ingram
General manager Christine Whiston
Editorial director (WW) Deborah Thomas

Produced by ACP Books, Sydney.
Printing by Times Printers Pte Ltd,
16 Tuas Avenue 5, Singapore 639340
Published by ACP Magazines Ltd,
54 Park St, Sydney;
GPO Box 4088, Sydney, NSW 2001
phone +61 2 9282 8618 fax +61 2 9267 9438
acpbooks@acpmagazines.com.au
www.acpbooks.com.au
To order books phone 136 116 (within Australia)
Send recipe enquiries to
recipeenquiries@acpmagazines.com.au

RIGHTS ENQUIRIES
Laura Bamford, Director ACP Books
lbamford@acpmedia.co.uk

Australia Distributed by Network Services,
phone +61 2 9282 8777 fax +61 2 9264 3278
networkweb@networkservicescompany.com.au
United Kingdom Distributed by Australian
Consolidated Press (UK),
phone (01604) 497 531 fax (01604) 497 533
books@acpmedia.co.uk
Canada Distributed by Whitecap Books Ltd,
phone (604) 980 9852 fax (604) 980 8197
customerservice@whitecap.ca
www.whitecap.ca
New Zealand Distributed by Netlink
Distribution Company,
phone (9) 366 9966 ask@ndc.co.nz
South Africa Distributed by PSD Promotions,
phone (27 11) 392 6065/6/7
fax (27 11) 392 6079/80
orders@psdprom.co.za

The Australian Women's Weekly
Play and learn
Includes index.
ISBN-13 978-1-86396-560-6
ISBN-10 1 86396 560 2.
1. Handicraft – Juvenile literature.
2. Creative activities and seat work – Juvenile
literature. I. Title. II. Title: Play and learn.
III. Title: Australian Women's Weekly.
745.5
© ACP Magazines Ltd 2006
ABN 18 053 273 546

Cover photography Getty Images